GOSSAMER

by
Stephen Cosgrove
Illustrated by
Wendy Edelson

MULTNOMAH

10209 SE Division Street, Portland, Oregon 97266

Library of Congress Cataloging-in Publication Data

Cosgrove, Stephen.
    Gossamer

    Summary: An encounter with a tattered and blind
butterfly helps the lovely winter weasel Prettina understand
the perils of vanity and the value of inner beauty.
    [1. Pride and vanity—Fiction. 2. Weasels—Fiction.
3. Butterflies—Fiction] I. Edelson, Wendy, ill. II. Title
PZ7.C8117Gp 1988   [E]   88-25531

©1988 by Stephen Cosgrove
Published by Multnomah Press
Portland, Oregon 97266
Printed in USA
All Rights Reserved.
ISBN 0-88070-241-9

91 92 93 94 95 96 97 98 - 9 8 7 6 5 4 3 2

To my favorite word-whacker
Jane Aldrich Brown.

arther than far and to the very edge of the horizon was a path bordered in snow-covered lacy fern. If you walked down that path following the snow steps of creatures who went before, you would find a land called Barely There.

Barely There . . . a crystal, snowy land filled with the magic and delight of winter's white drape. Hardy shoots of green had begun to pop through the snows of winter past, and the air was full of the promise of spring.

The paths, well worn by winter, show traces of fallen leaves blended with yellowed winter grasses. All of this would have been a dismal scene had it not been for the frost and snow, a gentle winter glaze. Trees that had lost their foliage were painted in crystal colors of ice and blue.

Most of the creatures of Barely There—the bears and others of their kind—had long since filled their bellies with good things to eat, put on their night shirts, and had fallen fast asleep.

But this was winter in the land of Barely There, a magical place indeed. Instead of being sad at the loss of summer's life, most of the forest creatures were glad, and they relished the gentle bite of winter's touch. For in winter's dying came the promise of spring's rebirth.

There lived in this part of Barely There a winter weasel called Prettina. She was the prettiest creature in the Land of Barely There, or at least she thought she was.

Her coat was velvet white with bits of purple that tipped her royal fur. Her nose was pink and pert and sniffed the gentle breeze for a whiff of perfume that might signal the coming of spring. Her ebony eyes

gazed into the morning mists searching for a bit of this or a bit of that to reflect her beauty.

For, you see, Prettina liked to compare herself to all the animals in the Land of Barely There. Dashing here and there she searched for another creature that might be as pretty as she.

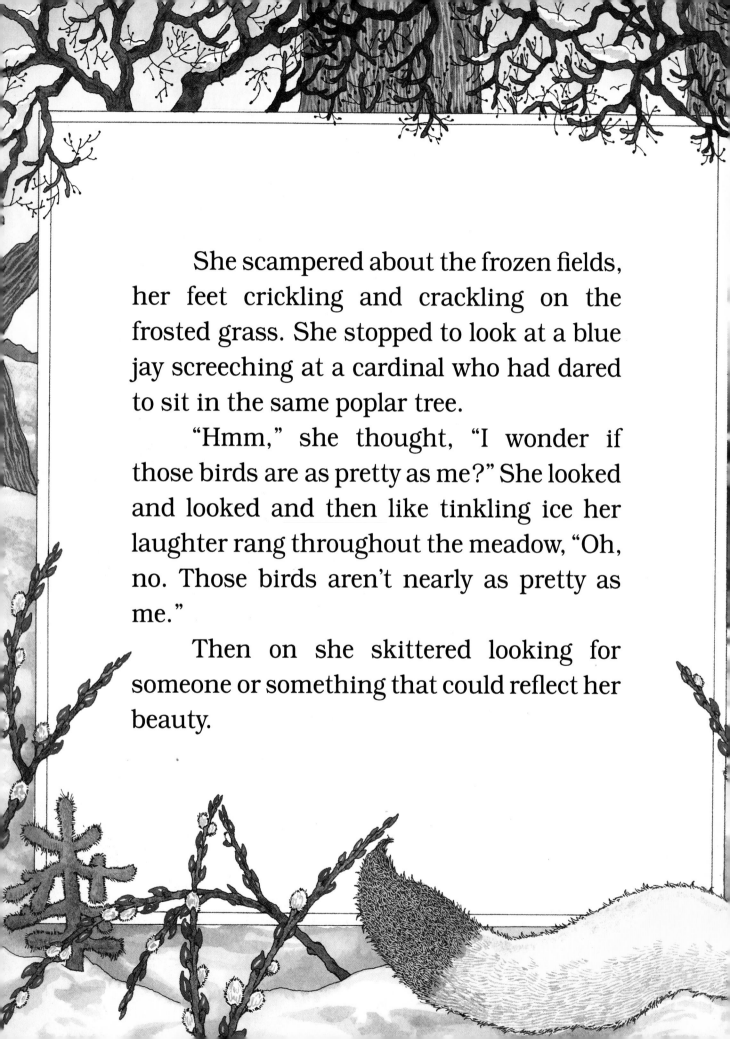

She scampered about the frozen fields, her feet crickling and crackling on the frosted grass. She stopped to look at a blue jay screeching at a cardinal who had dared to sit in the same poplar tree.

"Hmm," she thought, "I wonder if those birds are as pretty as me?" She looked and looked and then like tinkling ice her laughter rang throughout the meadow, "Oh, no. Those birds aren't nearly as pretty as me."

Then on she skittered looking for someone or something that could reflect her beauty.

She ran across the crystal meadow
just as the sun danced its rainbows from the
frozen dew. On and on she ran singing a
simple song. *"I'm so pretty, so pretty can't
you see. Is there anyone in Barely There
who is as pretty as me?"*

Her simple song was rudely inter-
rupted by three chipmunks sitting on the
limb of a pitchy pine tree. "Here we are,

Prettina," they laughed and teased. "We are as pretty as thee . . . can't you see?" They posed and primped as they chattered from the tree.

"Don't be silly," she laughed. "Chubby little chipmunks as pretty as me?" With that, she vainly pirouetted in a flurry of frost and rime.

Prettina hadn't gone very far when she came upon some bunnies rooting about in the snow, looking for hidden winter carrots. She stopped and laughed as she sang her simple song, *"I'm so pretty, so pretty can't you see. Is there anyone in Barely There who is as pretty as me?"*

"I know where there is someone as pretty as thee," said one of the rabbits as he crunched and munched on a bunch of carrots.

"As pretty as me?" she asked in horror. "Where is there someone as pretty as me?"

The rabbit continued his munching and slyly said, "Go to Mirror Lake, and there, just at the water's edge, you will find someone as pretty as thee. Best be careful, for the ice is as thin as your vanity."

Prettina, not listening to his warning, cried "It's a lie! There can be no one as pretty as me."

She ran and ran until she came to Mirror Lake. Pausing for a moment to catch her breath, she fluffed her hair, put on her prettiest smile, and leaned over the frozen lake to gaze at whatever was as pretty as she. There she saw the blurry outline of a winter weazel all white and furry bright.

Prettina shook her head in fear and fright, "Oh, no! It is a creature as pretty as me." She began to run across the ice, but no matter how far she ran, whenever she looked down she could see the ghosted reflection of another creature just as pretty as she.

She ran and skittered across the ice, vainly trying to outrun her own reflection. She would have run all the way across the lake had not the ice become weakened by the early spring sun. Long black lines zigged and zagged all around her as the ice began to rumble.

Prettina leaped just as the ice cracked and she landed in a heap on a tiny island right in the center of Mirror Lake. There she sat, afraid of her own reflection.

She would have been there to this very day if there had not come a fluttering in the sky. Flipping and flapping with rag-tag wings flew a very old and tattered butterfly.

"Is there someone there?" he said as he floated about.

The little winter weasel looked about and said, "I am here, old butterfly. Who are you?"

With his torn wings flopping, he dropped with a bump to the island. "I am called Gossamer," he said in an old weathered voice. "I have been looking for autumn, but I seem to have flown right by it. Now I have flown past winter and am nearing spring. Why are you on this island?"

Prettina's tears dripped down her cheeks as she told Gossamer how she came to be on the rock in the middle of Mirror Lake.

Gossamer laughed and laughed when she finished her tale.

"I don't think there is anything to laugh about," sniffed Prettina as she stifled a sob.

"Oh, my dear little weasel, I am not laughing at you but at the remembrance of another story. Listen as I tell you . . ."

Once there was the most beautiful butterfly in all the Land of Barely There. At first he didn't know that he was beautiful, but one day he happened to fly over a

sparkling creek. He looked down and saw the most beautiful creature he had ever seen. It was then that the butterfly realized he was looking at his mirrored image. So enamored was he, that from that day forward he looked most everywhere to see his own reflection.

Gossamer paused as he wiped his eyes with his tattered wings.

He was so much in love with his own image that he hated to see the sun set, for at night there was little or no reflection.

One night, as he was flying high above the clouds, he looked below and saw a flash and a spark. Knowing for certain that where there was light there was reflection he dove hungrily toward the source. His butterfly body twisted and turned as he recklessly flew downward.

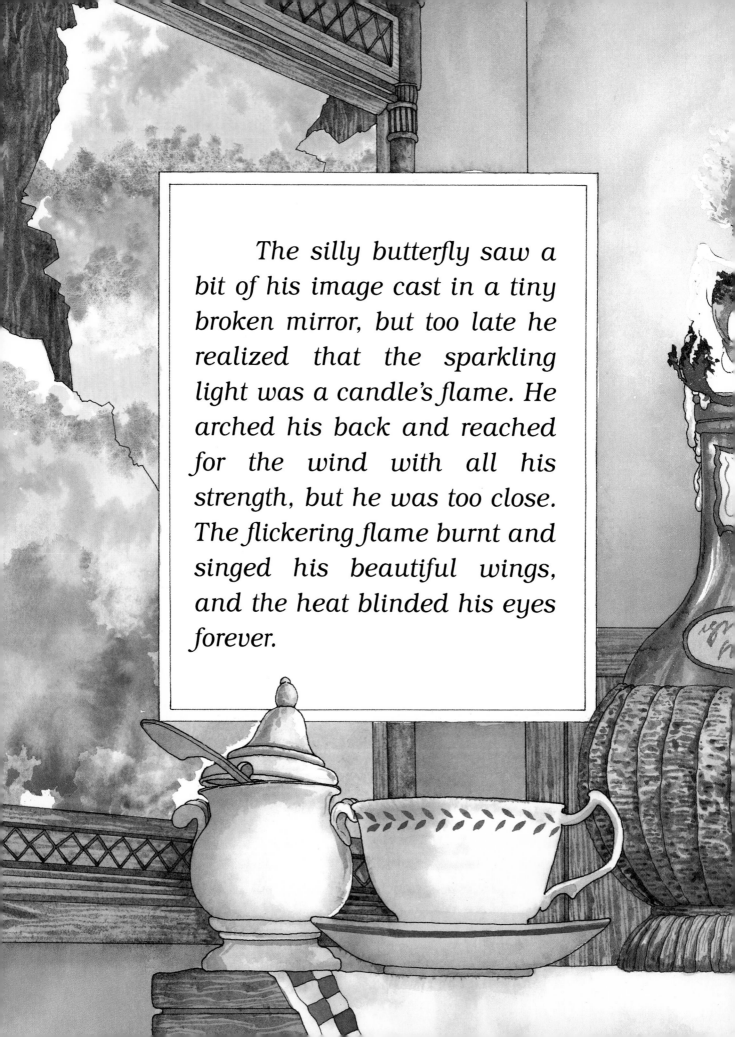

The silly butterfly saw a bit of his image cast in a tiny broken mirror, but too late he realized that the sparkling light was a candle's flame. He arched his back and reached for the wind with all his strength, but he was too close. The flickering flame burnt and singed his beautiful wings, and the heat blinded his eyes forever.

"Oh, I am so sorry," said Prettina. Her heart filled with pity as she realized that Gossamer was telling his own story.

The old butterfly fluttered his wings and gently sat down on the winter weazel's nose. He chuckled, "Sorry? You feel sorry for me? No, my little Prettina, I feel sorry for you. It is true that I was blinded by the flame because of my vanity. But even though I cannot see, I'm not really blind. It's all in how

you feel about yourself. I'm having a glorious time finding the warmth of spring."

The little weasel's eyes crossed as she looked at the ugly rag-tag butterfly. Suddenly it dawned on her that in comparison he was far more beautiful than she. Though he appeared ugly on the outside because of his burnt and tattered wings, on the inside he was filled with love . . . and his beauty, as beauty must, glowed from deep within.

With Gossamer fluttering beside her, the humbled winter weasel carefully crossed icy Mirror Lake and guided the blind but beautiful butterfly back to spring and the Land of Barely There.

There they live to this very day, telling all the creatures in the land that outward beauty can be enjoyed only when inward beauty is present.

Other books
in this series

Derby Downs
Fiddler
Hannah & Hickory
Ira Wordworthy
Persimmony
Shadow Chaser
T.J. Flopp